C000259592

Images of
LEICESTER

Leicester Mercury

Images of
LEICESTER

First published in Great Britain by The Breedon Books Publishing Company Limited 44 Friar Gate, Derby, DE1 1DA. 1995. Reprinted in Paperback 2004

This edition published in Great Britain in 2011 by The Derby Books Publishing Company Limited3 The Parker Centre, Derby, DE21 4SZ

© Leicester Mercury 1995

All Rights Reserved. No part of this publication may be reproduced, stored in a retrieval system, or transmitted in any form, or by any means, electronic, mechanical, photocopying, recording or otherwise without the prior permission in writing of the Copyright holders, nor be otherwise circulated in any form or binding or cover other than in which it is published and without a similar condition being imposed on the subsequent publisher.

ISBN 978-1-85983-919-5

Printed and bound by Melita Press, Malta.

Contents

Before 1900

An ornate flooring found on a Roman site near King Richard's Road. It is thought it shows an adventure of Cyparissus, a youth of Cea.

Mr Theodore Sturge, assistant keeper (conservation) at Leicester Museums, at work on the tessellated Roman pavement beneath the old Great Central Railway Station.

Lead coffins from Roman times being removed from under the former Great Central Railway Station in 1976 to allow the Roman pavement to be moved to the Jewry Wall Museum.

The medieval Town Walls, off Sanvey Gate, pictured in 1938.

Leicester's first library, in the Town Hall, now the Guildhall.

Above and below: The Chantry House of St George at 18 Highcross Street, which may be contemporary with William Wigston's Chantry House in the Newarke, which was built in 1512 for the priests who served the Newarke Church. It survived the reformation, the siege and a near-miss from a German bomb in 1940.

Plaque at Chantry House of St George.

Leicester's Old Corn Exchange, sometimes known as the New Gainsborough, was built in 1747 and lasted for 103 years. Its upper rooms were used by the magistrates.

The interior of Leicester Castle as it was in 1821. This is where Parliament deliberated in Leicester in 1414, 1426 and 1450.

A drawing published in 1793. Traders are seen with their pack animals at the top of Welford Road Hill.

Highcross Street, pictured around 1830. Thornton Lane is shown as a narrow passage.

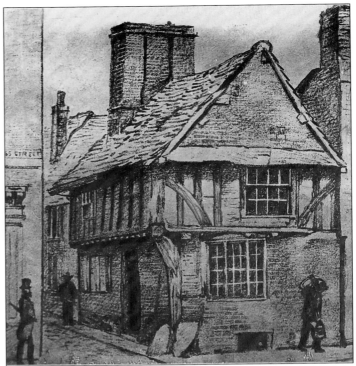

West Bridge Station pictured in 1832.

Leicester's Belgrave Road (Great Northern Railway) Station.

1995 is the 155th anniversary of the opening of the first Midland Railway station, with one platform, on Campbell Street. Note the Doric columns, designed by William Flint (1801-1862). It was demolished in 1892.

Commissioned officers of the 1st Leicestershire Militia around 1850.

Bow Bridge in the winter of about 1854.

16 August 1995 was the 140th anniversary of Thomas Cook's first excursion to the continent. His 'Pleasure Voyages and Travels' began with a 4.40pm train from Bishopsgate Street to Harwich and then by special streamer to Antwerp, for which a first class and best cabin cost 40 shillings. Thomas Cook's Granby Street Commercial Temperance Hotel (shown here) was Leicester's Food Office during World War One.

The last stage coach which left the Three Crowns Hotel in Leicester in 1860.

Horsefair Street in 1865.

London Road in 1866, from Victoria Park. The building in the foreground is the Marquis of Granby public house.

On 16 March 1868, the cornerstone was laid for the new Clock Tower by Mr John Burton at the spot known as Coal Hill.

Horsefair Street in 1868, before the Town Hall was built. Opposite the wagon is the old cattle market, which was removed to allow for the building of the Town Hall and Square, which was officially opened in 1876.

A view from St Martin's spire in 1869 showing a forest of chimneys belonging to small hosiery firms. High Street runs diagonally from left to right.

Top-hatted policemen on duty in the Haymarket before the Clock Tower was built in 1868.

An 1862 view of Eastgates.

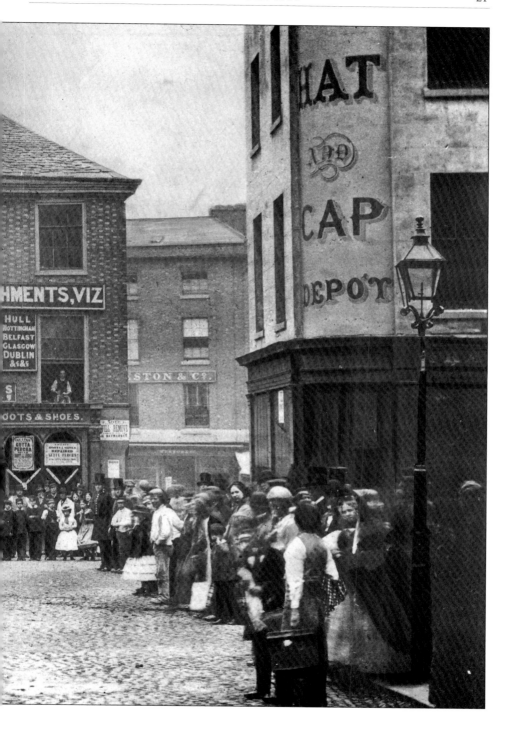

Welford Road Cemetery pictured about the year 1870.

Leicester's first horse-drawn tramcar at the Belgrave terminus in 1874.

William Green Payne standing in the doorway of his premises, 44 High Street, nearly opposite Huntingdon Tower, in around 1875. It was close to the entrance of the Royal Arcade.

London Road-Victoria Park Road corner in 1877, when there was no Mayfield Road. The Toll Gate and House were built 26 years earlier.

Half-timbered house at the corner of Highcross Street and Thornton Lane, which was demolished when the Golden Lion public house was rebuilt around 1880.

Another view of Highcross Street taken in 1890.

An 1880s picture of Horsefair Street with a neatly turned-out policeman.

An audience paused from watching a Punch and Judy show to smile at the photographer. The scene is the Corn Exchange in about 1880.

Applegate Street:
L.P.North's meat stores,
between 1882 and 1888. In
later years it was occupied
by Hornbuckle, butchers. A
directory of 1888 shows
W.H. Smith at No 12, which
should be the opposite side
of the street.

A horse-bus on the West Bridge – picture was taken from the railway bridge which crosses the canal at Bath Lane.

Horse-drawn tramcar No.19 on London Road in the 1890s. The church, next to the railway station, is St Stephen's Presbyterian, which was demolished in 1894.

Below and opposite page: The arch erected in the Haymarket for the visit of the Prince and Princess of Wales (the future Edward VII and his wife, Alexandra) to open the Abbey Park on 29 May 1882. The second arch was at the end of Campbell Street. The building depicted through the archway is Granville House, the home of Henry Thornhill, HM Inspector of Factories. A few years later, it was the home of George Jessop, a prominent engineer and then Midland Hotel.

Above and opposite page, top: Two views of Bridge Street looking from Castle Street towards the Mitre and Keys Inn, around late 1880s or early 1890s. In the first picture, the building with the gable end is the famous bakery of Elizabeth and Charlotte Perkins. The second shows the Royal Oak, Richard Flude's hairdresser, fishing tackle dealer and tobacconist, then Pinks dyers and cleavers, and finally Mrs Sarah Shipley, who was fruiterer and florist.

The Methodist New Connexion Chapel, in St Paul's Methodist Church, standing on the site of the London Road Railway Station, with Corinthian pillars. The church was rebuilt in Melbourne Road at the corner of Dale Street after 1892, but finally closed in 1963. The pillars were relocated to the façade of Mr Arthur Wakerley's rubber factory at the corner of Leicester Street and Rolleston Street.

The chemist's shop of Mr Alf Berridge at its original site on the corner of Cheapside and Cank Street, around 1889. The business was later moved to the opposite corner.

Victorian citizens obligingly posing for the cameraman at the corner of Eastgate and New Bond Street. Hams are hung at the front of Johnson's provisions store.

The city's celebrations for Queen Victoria's Diamond Jubilee included the planting of an oak tree in Victoria Park (22 June 1897).

Huntingdon's Tower on High Street, which was demolished in 1902, when the street was widened for the introduction of electric trams. Only one of two towers in the mansion, called Lord's Place, survived. It was the town house of Henry Hastings, third Earl of Huntingdon. He bought it in 1569 from two brothers, John and Ralph Eaton. Its grounds extended from East Bond Street to Union Street. Mary Queen of Scots and Charles I stayed there.

Clock Tower scene showing the East Gates Coffee House.

East Gates around
1898.

The opening of Newarke Bridge on 24 October 1898. In the first carriage rides the Mayor, Councillor Arthur Wakerley.

This house stood in St Nicholas Street until the year 1899. John Bunyan lodged here and the Revd John Wesley stayed when a guest of Mr Coltman. The local school, conducted by Miss Emma Poppleton, was at 26 St Nicholas Street.

Two views of Halford Street. The wholesale market pre-1914 and the Masonic Hall in 1859, which became the Coventry Arms. When the pub closed at the end of 1964, the Co-operative Permanent Building Society extended into it

Above and opposite page: The little conservatory perched above the ground floor of a shop was not an unusual architectural feature in the last century. This one is at 69 High Street, the Co-operative Society's tea-rooms, in 1900. Earlier, it was Stephen Cooper's dining and refreshment rooms (second picture). The building was demolished to make way for electric trams in 1904.

Wellington Hotel seen
from Granby Street,
pre-1900.

Below: Leicester Royal Infirmary as it was in 1876. The view is from Welford Road and the steeple is that of St Mary's Church. The walled building on the left was the asylum, which was used until the county asylum was opened in 1836.

An old drawing gives some idea of the state of Abbey Park before it was transformed for the opening in 1882.

Joseph Aloysius Hansom, who designed a patent safety cab, also designed Leicester's Nonconformist Proprietary School in New Walk in 1836. The building is now the Leicestershire Museum and Art Gallery.

The grandstand at the Victoria Park racecourse in the 1860s. The building later became a pavilion.

Early Years of the Century

Bedford Street, Leicester, showing the Tramway Inn at No 7, just in from Belgrave Gate. Earlier, in 1880 it was known as the Tram Inn and was demolished around the turn of the century.

The Admiral Duncan in Fleet Street at the turn of the century. Fleet Street ran from Bedford Street to Dryden Street.

The entrance to the Market Place early 1900s.

The passage of the years has left Leicester's Narborough Road surprisingly untouched by progress as this picture taken in the early years of this century clearly shows. Of particular interest is the chapel on the right of the picture and the early open-topped electric tram.

King Street at the beginning of the century. The house on the extreme left has now gone, its site now a flower planted triangle. Earlier it was the Edinburgh Hotel with proprietor George Waddington, then Waddington's Temperance Hotel, run by Louise and Annie Waddington.

This delightful Frog Island scene, from the pre-1904 days of horse-drawn trams, has so many interesting details, including the Frear's delivery van (outside the bakery and shop) and a host of street signs.

How the bread was delivered before motorised transport came about. This pre-World War One picture shows a horse and wagon belonging to Squires Bakery of Narborough Road.

Winn's Oriental Cafe and Spencer's Library in the Market Place, in about 1900.

Fosse Road North in the early 1900s.

St Nicholas Street at the turn of the century.

High Street in 1901. Note the Huntingdon Tower, which was encased in brick.

The Talbot Inn, West Bridge, pictured in 1901.

Charles and Frank Haines, Johnny Mott and Bert Riley, the 'Hamorils' music, mirth and melody pierrots, in 1901.

Leicester Fosse FC players in 1901-02, when they were runners–up in the Leicestershire Senior Cup, losing to Hinckley 3-1. Back row (left to right): Brown (trainer), Boulston, Dainty, Webb, Richards, Mr W. Smith (director). Middle row: Marshall, Mills, Swift (captain), Daw, Gill, Mr G. Johnson (secretary). Front row: Robinson, Brown, King.

Coronation Day, 9 August 1902. The town celebrated King Edward VII's Coronation with a procession, amusements on the parks and fireworks. This scene is in Gallowtree Gate.

Robert Monk, proprietor of the Robin Hood Hotel in Gallowtree Gate, also decorated his premises to celebrate the Coronation.

This was the view in High Street in 1902, when the rails were being placed for Leicester's new electric trams, and the old narrow east-to-west High Street-St Nicholas Street was widened to allow for a double tram track without obstruction to other wheeled traffic.

The Clock Tower in the electric tramway siege of 1903.

Track-laying at the junction of Welford Road and Clarendon Park Road 1903.

Preparing for electric trams at the Evington Road-London Road corner, around 1902 or 1903.

Granby Street and Calais Hill Junction, preparing for the tram lines to be laid, 1904.

The official opening of Leicester's electric trams on 18 May 1904.

August Bank Holiday Show at the Abbey Park in 1905, when B.B.Kieran won the half–mile English Championship, swimming along the River Soar.

View of Narborough Road junction in 1905.

The imposing figure of Tubby Stephens, who achieved pre-eminence rarely given to a constable. PC 83 John William Stephens, was England's heaviest constable around the turn of the century, weighing in at more than 24 stones.

Staff of the Leicester Lunatic Asylum, which was built in 1837 on a site at the top of Knighton Hill. A new asylum was opened in Narborough in 1907. During World War One it was used as a military hospital. In 1918 it was bought by T. Fielding Johnson and presented to the university college.

Amelia Marlow Sherwin and her mother Sarah Ann Sherwin in the doorway of their tripe shop at the corner of Fairfax Street and Mill Lane in about 1903. It was demolished in the mid–1950s.

Until recently, the last Leicester Fair held in Humberstone Gate was in May 1904.

Queen's Road, near the junction with Clarendon Park Road, in 1906.

A scene in High Street before 1905. The shop is Payne's, a dealer in game, which would give today's health inspectors cause for concern.

Two scenes of Gallowtree Gate, around 1910.

Above and previous page: Mr Ramsay MacDonald canvassing in the Market Place and Willow Street in 1906.

Jackson's the Hatters of 28 Gallowtree Gate in about 1910.

Welford Road, around 1910.

The Victoria Park Pavilion *c.*1910. It was destroyed by a land mine in November 1940.

The scene before the Granby Halls Leisure Centre was built at the junction of Welford Road and Aylestone Road in 1910. The Granby Halls were initially the Junior Training Halls to meet the needs of World War One.

Service commemorating the Coronation of King George V, held in the Market Place on 22 June 1911.

Scenes from the great St George's Church fire on 5 October 1911.

A horse and dray used to deliver gas cookers for the Corporation of Leicester Gas and Coke Co. from the Aylestone Road works.

Moat Road school class in 1912. Recognise anyone?

The call to arms is heard in Leicester during early August, 1914. Mostly young men volunteer at the Magazine. All wear smiles ... it'll all be over by Christmas!

London Road Railway Station during World War One with troops boarding a train for the front.

A remarkable picture portraying the life of the period during the beginning of World War One in Leicester. Life goes on but there is the constant reminder of the far-off battle. The elderly gentlemen pilots his horse and trap through the milling pedestrians, a smart young lad, complete with buttonhole, trots past the tea stores at the Central buildings approach to Leicester Market Place. Dominating this particular scene is the flag-seller and his partner – a sailor and a nurse – and (who could ever resist a uniform) a buyer.

Two policemen keep order at a
queue outside a butcher's shop
in Welford Road during World
War One.

Mrs Nellie Wayte, the
manageress, pictured at the
front of Samuel Hurst's Great
Northern Boot Stores at 141
Belgrave Road during
World War One.

A May Day procession in 1916
around the Clock Tower.

Their Majesties King George V
and Queen Mary enter the state
carriage at London Road Railway
Station on a state visit in June
1919.

The date: 19 July 1919. The place: Clarendon Park. The occasion: celebrating peace and victory in costumes.

The Twenties

George Henton's suggestion for the layout of Castle Gardens in 1920. The main feature was the terracing down to the banks.

The 'cast' of the 1920 Mayflower Festival held in Leicester to mark the 300th anniversary of the Pilgrim Fathers setting sail for America.

A photographer's and artist's studio stood on the corner of London Road and Conduit Street pictured about 1920 and now sadly gone. To the side is the railway station.

The site of Burton's tailoring establishment — Allen and Co, wine and spirit merchants, on the corner of Humberstone Gate and Gallowtree Gate, which was demolished around 1926.

Leicester folk still regard Kemp's clock with affection, for many people have stood under it waiting for their sweetheart or friend to meet them there, this scene was taken in the 1920s.

Houses in the 1920s with overcrowding and poverty a grim reality.

A scene in Knighton now changed, the houses are gone but the Cradock Arms remains.

Belgrave Gate in the 1920s, before Charles Street had been thought of. By 1930 the whole of the eastern side from Charles Street to the Great Northern station had been demolished. A drinking fountain, which stood at the Old Cross, at the site of the traffic island at the entrance to Charles Street, is now in the museum.

Narborough Road railway bridge before widening. The work commenced 26 August 1928 and took until 6 September.

The Thirties

Charles Street, as it was in 1930 before widening, looking from Rutland Street. The site on the left was to become the municipal offices. The Queen's Hotel was demolished and rebuilt on the opposite corner.

A Hansom cab and the Clock Tower in the 1930s – a re-enactment.

The last meeting of the City Council in the old chamber in 1932.

The Pageant of Leicester took place between 16-28 June 1932. It was organised by Mr Frank Lascelles and was attended by 118,815 people. It was the brainchild of Councillor Charles E. Gillott, not to particularly commemorate any one event, although it did coincide with the 50th anniversary of the opening of Abbey Park. The much-improved Charles Street opened on 21 June and was designated Leicester Civic Day. Britain was still in the grip of the depression and the pageant greatly raised morale.

Scenes from the Leicester Pageant. Cardinal Wolsey, preceded by the Abbott, walking to his last sanctuary in the Abbey.

Lady Ethelfleda's Army.

'Daniel Lambert' (Sgt Hankinson) greets the Lord Mayor of Leicester, (Alderman W.E. Wilford) at the Guildhall in the 1932 Leicester Pageant.

A scene from the Leicester Pageant in 1932 – Rupert's Gateway.

The opening of Charles Street on 21 June 1932.

The cake shop at 48 Hinckley Road in 1933. A large loaf cost 4½d (2p) in those days.

A 1935 picture of St Nicholas Street. The buildings on the right were demolished to make way for new public baths. Excavations, however, revealed some Roman remains and, instead of the baths, we now have the Forum.

Corner of Campbell Street and Charles Street.

Usherettes outside the Picture House
in the 1930s.

W.T.Mills, Ironmongers, opened in
East Park Road in 1935, when the
average weekly wage was 53s 3d
(£2.66).

Belgrave Road, Melton Road and Loughborough Road junction in the mid-1930s. The cars pictured, left to right, are a Standard saloon, what appears to be a bull-nose Morris, a check-grilled Vauxhall and an Austin Ten saloon.

Chief Constable Mr O.J.B.Cole with his deputy, Supt John Gabbitas, leads his force in a parade from the new headquarters in Charles Street on the occasion of the force's centenary in February 1936.

The Charles Street Municipal Offices in the course of construction in 1937.

The Newarke Gateway and Magazine seen here before World War Two with people waiting for their buses. Note the inspector checking his watch.

Granby Street on 20 September 1937, illustrating concern over road traffic in the city centre.

Christening of the
Leicestershire Regiment
engine at the Fox Street
sidings in March 1938,
commemorating the 250th
anniversary of the Leicesters.
Driver T.A.Green and
Fireman G.Clement had
both served in the regiment.

Causeway Lane at the corner with Highcross Street, part of the site for 'new proposed central swimming baths' on 19 May 1938.

A late 18th-century house in Sanvey Gate in July 1938. John Henry Hardy ran a butcher's business at No. 43 and next door, at 41c, was William Cave, a boot and shoe dealer, then at 41b, Mrs Ida Cooke, a grocer.

The scene at the new stretch of road which would eliminate the 'S' bend at the tram terminus in Groby Road in August 1938.

The scene inside a pre-war provisions store in Hotel Street, possibly R.L.Ackinson at No.18, a Stilton house.

Gallowtree Gate looking towards Granby Street just prior to World War Two.

A City at War

A 2/5th Leicesters recruitment meeting in June 1939, with a bren carrier.

Training for women tram conductors in February 1940.

Cavendish Road, which suffered Leicester's first bombing in August 1940.

Members of the Home Guard receiving instruction on the use of the Lewis gun in October 1940.

The stark shell of Freeman, Hardy and Willis premises in Rutland Street on 19 November 1940.

An officer taking the salute during the march past of the Home Guard in December 1940.

Taylor, Taylor and Hobson, a new binocular works in the Midlands in January 1941. Mrs Fuller, Mrs Wild and Miss Osborne are newcomers to the industry.

Large ovens at the Ministry of Food Emergency cooking depot at Humberstone, where food for British Restaurants and schools were prepared in 1942.

Twice a day London Midland and Scottish Railways van girls would travel from Campbell Street to collect and deliver to shops and banks in 1941.

Mrs J.Stonehewer, of the Ford Emergency Food Vans Trust, hands to the Lord Mayor (Councillor Miss Frisby) the keys to the emergency food vans which Mr Henry Ford has presented to Leicestershire in February 1942.

The Ministry of Food Advice Bureau in Charles Street. A lady visitor is being shown a wartime pudding.

Partridge Wilson's factory on Pike Street during World War Two.

Mrs Burbidge on duty with the National Fire Service during World War Two.

The Americans brought their own sporting enthusiasm to Leicester. A baseball match at Abbey Park, watched by US servicemen in August 1943.

All ready for a good meal at an evacuees' receiving centre in the city.

This page and next page: VE Day 8 May 1945, and Leicester celebrates the end of the war in Europe, with parades, a Clock Tower conga, and street parties. The one pictured is on Ridley Street.

Post-War Days

New lamp standards for Leicester in 1947. The view at Northampton Square.

London Road Railway Station, before the last tram and at the time of the introduction of buses.

London Road / East Street area in March 1948.

John Bigg's statue stood proud in Welford Place on 20 January 1949, soon to be replaced by an 'L' shaped traffic island, so that traffic from Belvoir Street could filter into Pocklington's Walk.

Leicester lights up – the Clock Tower scene on a Saturday night in April 1949.

Knocking off time – workers travelling home at the junction of MacDonald Road and Belgrave Road in the late 1940s.

Leicester City's Filbert Street ground after the restoration of the stand, 9 August 1949.

On 9 November 1949, Leicester said farewell to its last electric tram, after the introduction of the service 45 years earlier.

Leicester's biggest chimney, the 210ft, 60-year-old stack at the old Leicester tram department power station in Painter Street, was being demolished brick by brick in November 1949.

The Fifties

The removal of tramlines in High Street in 1950. Trams had ceased running the previous year.

The Hinckley Road-Narborough Road junction.

Hinckley Road junction with Wyngate Drive, in the years following World War Two.

Leicester's wholesale fruit market was always a bustling hive of activity especially in the early hours of the morning with produce arriving from all over Britain and the world. Sadly, it has since gone the way of many other fine buildings.

June 1951. Shell-B.P. House near the London Road Railway Station which was The Old Wyvern Hotel. Nowadays the site houses a multi-storey block of flats.

The New Walk at King Street on a damp day in September 1951. Trinity Church stands in the background.

Looking along Humberstone Gate beyond the Charles Street crossing. The view was taken in June 1951 from Lewis's store tower, the only part of the building still standing today.

A panoramic view taken from Lewis's Tower showing Charles Street and beyond Lee Street Circle later to become a multi-storey car park.

Leicester Hunters speedway team became the first holders of the Midland Cup, defeating Birmingham in October 1951. The Hunters later became the Leicester Lions.

Ye Old Pack Horse in Belgrave Gate, demolished to make way for the flyover, even though the date on the front door says it all – it had been there since 1539. Only the pub name survived, transferred to a new building in Belgrave Gate.

The Saracen's Head on the corner of Hotel Street and Market Place South has changed little since it was built in 1901. The view was taken in December 1951.

The Old Black Lion in Yeoman Street, off Humberstone Gate, has changed little since this picture was taken in 1951.

School days back in June 1952 at Church of Christ the King on Glenfield Road.

The Cathedral, St Martin's, pictured from New Street, in September 1952.

The Common, Evington, which was to be purchased by the Corporation for development as a shopping quarter, community centre, car-park and library. Pack Lane is on the left and Cordery Road to the right.

Leicestershire opencast coal being bagged at West Bridge Wharf in February 1953.

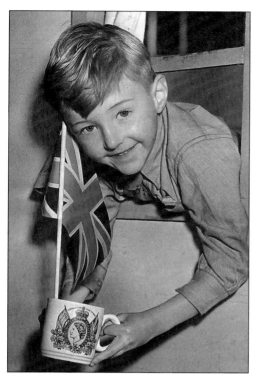

Peter Taylor is very pleased with life – and he has every reason to be, for his fifth birthday fell on Coronation Day 1953. He is pictured looking through the window of the nursery house at the Mantle Road Infants School, after receiving his Coronation mug.

St Peter's Road and St Stephen's Road junction in June 1953, Coronation Year.

Nicknamed 'Old Calow the Sweep', Alfred Calow was still working at the grand old age of 82.

The *Evening Mail* offices in July 1954 on London Road; the newspaper ceased publication in 1963.

A 1954 view of the canal looking towards Frog Island Bridge.

The bridge at Western Boulevard with Castle Gardens in the background – the scene has changed little since this picture in February 1955.

Horsefair Street, in March 1955, Brucciani the well known coffee shop and ice cream parlour is alas no more, as neither are G.A.Sykes and Gollands. The police allowed parking in those days in the Town Hall Square.

Leicester's Clock Tower, built in 1868, is the city's best known landmark.

The National Westminster Bank in St Martin's in March 1955. This was formerly the site of Parr's Bank.

That famous brand name 'Wolsey' had their offices in King Street, now the site is the Leicester New Walk Centre.

Applegate Street in March 1955. These shops made way for the Holiday Inn.

Stock cars roar around the track at Leicester Speedway Stadium in Blackbird Road in 1955. This was also the home of Leicester Lions speedway team.

Fosse Road North in April 1955. The main forms of transport seem to be cycles and 'Shank's pony'.

A busy Humberstone Gate in June 1955. The Bell Hotel is on the left.

Children leaving Moat Road School make their way down St Saviour's Road to East Park Road with Spinney Hill Park on the left behind the trees, 30 June 1955.

De Montfort Square with the land used for the council's kitchen garden, pictured in August 1955. Now the area is surrounded by offices.

The old fire station in Rutland Street in October 1955. It made way for Leicester City Corporation's bus offices.

The Empire Hotel on Fosse Road North with St Augustine's Church to the left in October 1955.

King Richard's Road, pictured from Tudor Road corner, in October 1955.

Charles Street in November 1955 with the electricity offices in the foreground. The space to the right is now the Alliance and Leicester Building Society.

Seen on a cold, misty day in December 1955, The Newarkes with, on the left the
College of Art and Technology; on the right, Newarke houses with St Mary de Castro
Church peering through the winter murk behind Rupert's Gateway.

February 1956. The National Provincial Bank on the corner of Granby Street and Horsefair Street, which later became the National Westminster Bank.

The winter sunshine reflects on the weir at Aylestone in February 1956.

The Wellington Hotel in the city centre. In 1957 the 130-year-old building was set for a face lift, involving the installation of shops on the ground floor.

Waiting to use the telephone box – a young lady stands admiring a beautiful flower bed at the end of New Walk at Victoria Park in July 1957.

Knighton in 1958 with the Cradock Arms in the foreground. The grand house behind has now gone, in its place stand a dozen new houses.

This view taken in March 1958 looking down Granby Street from London Road; to the right is Northampton Square and Charles Street.

Tudor Road, April 1958, with its mixture of shops and houses.

Welford Road Cemetery Chapel, which was demolished in October 1958.

The Stag and Pheasant in Humberstone Gate, seen here in October 1958, went the way of many grand hotels and pubs, when the centre was redeveloped.

Holy Bones, in February 1959, so named after the discovery of animal bones found during excavations. These were the remains of sacrifices offered up by the Romans to the god Janus whose temple stood on the spot 2,000 years before.

The Floral Hall and Palace Theatre in The Haymarket in 1959.

The Swan with Two Necks public house on Granby Street, in March 1959. Notice the high ground floor and small upper storey.

Glenhills Boulevard on The Eyres Monsell Estate pictured in May 1959. Now a busy road cuts through the centre leading to the M1 and M69.

The Bishop Street Methodist Church, which celebrated its 180th anniversary in 1995. The church had come a long way since John Wesley addressed a crowd in a large room in High Street (now Highcross Street) in 1757. The plot was bought by the church in 1815, from an innkeeper, Alderman William Bishop, for £637 13s. The cost of building the church came to £4,900 and it was opened in August 1816. It is pictured here in 1959.

The country's first drive-in post office was opened in December 1959 at Wharf Street when the then Assistant Postmaster General, Miss Mervyn Pike, MP for Melton, became the first motorist customer.

This photograph (and previous picture) was taken in 1959, from the arch of the Newarke Gateway looking up Newarke Street. Notice the AEC Renown six-wheeler double-decker bus, one of which is preserved at Snibston Discovery Park.

A cattle trough on Narborough Road seen in 1959. It was placed there in 1903 by wealthy philanthropists, George and Annie Bills.

The Crescent on King Street. Happily, this fine building has been restored.

Parking scene in Granby Street at 10am, half an hour before the 'no waiting' restrictions came into affect on 25 July 1959. Nowadays there is no parking at all in this area.

The plaque on William Carey's cottage.

The old West Bridge Station in 1955.

School holidays in full swing and time for some boating in Abbey Park in July 1953.

Lord Mayor Alderman Sidney Brown spoke at the opening of the new Victoria Park pavilion on 10 December 1958.

The Queen, accompanied by the Duke of Edinburgh, paid her first visit to Leicester on 9 May 1958. She is welcomed by the Lord Mayor Alderman Frederick Jackson and his wife and is pictured with Mr R. L. Wessel, chairman of Corah's.

The Sixties

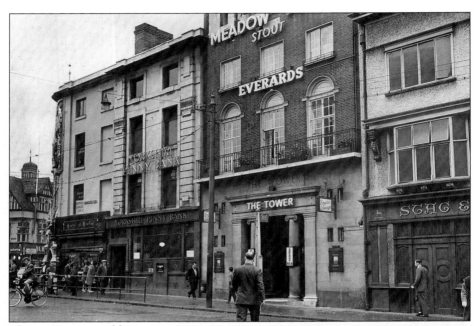

The Tower public house pictured in October 1960, later demolished to become Littlewood's store.

The first cattle market was held in the Market Place. In 1774 it was moved to Horsefair Street and from there to the Welford Road site in 1868. Around 135,000 stock passed through the market in 1960.

Gateway girls protest march seen at the Clock Tower.

The old City of Leicester Boys' School, Humberstone Gate, pictured in 1960. It was formerly the home of the Wyggeston Girls' School until 1929 and is now the headquarters of Age Concern Leicester, Clarence House.

The British Red Cross Society now occupies Thomas Cook's home, Thorncroft at 244 London Road.

Housewives in the area approved of the new Downing Drive shops in Evington in the early 1960s.

The Market Place in October 1960.

A Christmas Eve queue outside a pork pie shop in 1960 in the Market Place.

A plaque commemorating Queen Victoria's Diamond Jubilee. This one was pictured in 1960 above a shop in St Saviour's Road.

Uppingham Road in the early 1960s. The cars of the period are a Hillman Minx, Vauxhall Cresta, Ford Popular and a Standard Vanguard.

Tudor Road in September 1960. The Tudor public house is on the left.

Pictured in November 1960, this area of Southgates has now changed completely.

The Essoldo cinema on Granby Street pictured on a rainy day in November 1960.

A 1960 view of the Newarkes with the Newarke House Museum on the left and the now-demolished barracks on the right. The Gateway at the far end is the only part of the barracks remaining.

A scene showing Oxford Street from the Infirmary in November 1960. The Swan and Rushes public house still stands but many of the buildings on the right hand side have long gone.

The canal at Frog Island, North Mills in 1960.

On 6 April 1961 Leicester became the first place in the country to have traffic wardens taking to the streets . 'Park at your peril!'

St Margaret's Bus Station in 1961; now on the site stands a modern new coach and bus station.

The Lee Circle car park under construction in 1961. This multi-decker was then the largest self-parking car park in the country.

Demolition work in Syston Street – part of a programme to eradicate sub-standard areas of Leicester.

May 1961 shows The Bowling Green in Oxford Street, believed to be the oldest public house still surviving.

A bird's eye view of the Clock Tower and surrounding shops. Many have now gone to make way for new developments, Littlewoods is now situated at the bottom right of the picture.

Pictured in 1961 and looking like the set of *Open All Hours*. This hardware shop in Charnwood Street certainly has a varied selection of goods for sale. Pity the poor shop worker who had to put all these out every morning then take them down again at closing time.

Charnwood Street, June 1962, with Issitt's clothes shop with prices such as 8s 11d and 21s.

The narrow bridge in Knighton Fields Road East. Beyond the bridge stood the swimming baths, now sadly gone.

Allandale Road pictured in December 1962.

The Market Place in 1963. Leicester's oldest-established outfitters closed in March of that year.

Previous page and above: A view from Prospect Hill looking up and down Granby Avenue in North Evington in the early 1960s.

Lights on at the university engineering block in 1963 and a splendid subject for a night-time picture.

The London Road widening scheme was completed in September 1963.

The Melbourne cinema, seen here in February 1963, up for sale. The popularity of television had seen the demise of many small local cinemas.

All smiles at Filbert Street as the players hear the draw for the semi-finals of the FA Cup in April 1963. It was to be Liverpool at Hillsborough on 27 April.

Built in 1937, The Knighton Kinema in Welford Road closed its doors for the last time in November 1963. It was later demolished.

A view from Epic House looking down on Charles St with Humberstone Gate traversing it, in February 1964. Most of the area has now changed.

A 1964 view of
Leicester Market
Place.

Gallowtree Gate in November 1964. This area is now pedestrianised.

A motorist in a Mini stops to admire the Christmas lights at AEI in Melton Road in 1964. The windmills and thousands of coloured lights which are manufactured there make a scene reminiscent of Paris or Amsterdam.

Prince Rupert's Gateway forms an attractive frame for the ornamental lamps and the Newarke House Museum in this view from March 1965.

The lifting bridge designed by Robert Stephenson, son of the railway pioneer. The bridge, dating from 1834, spanned the Soar near West Bridge.

A bird's eye view of the Crescent in King Street in 1965.

School days, and children try out an educational aid made by Invicta Plastics, of Oadby. These mathematical balances were part of an order of 3,000 for West German schools.

The 'Troc' or Trocadero cinema and dance hall, where many young sweethearts met, pictured here in 1966, was demolished to make way for a petrol station.

The Old Original Tripe Shop, J.Biddles, in Humberstone Gate, Leicester, established in 1832 and still thriving in 1967.

Women sorting and cutting potatoes before they go into the slicing machine at Walker's Crisps factory in Barkby Road in March 1967.

An aerial view taken in
May 1967 showing work
proceeding with the St
Nicholas   Circle
development. The main
area in the centre was to
become the Holiday Inn.

A young woman at work
on a bar tacker at
R.Rowley & Co Ltd in
September 1967.

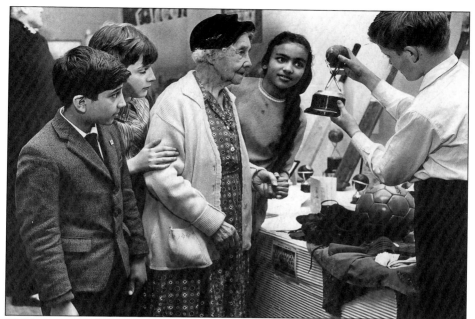

Children at Bridge School show 100-year-old Mrs Clara Ogden some sporting mementos at an exhibition on Leicester at their school in May 1968.

Leicester's Market Place, pictured before redevelopment, in May 1968.

Looking down on the junction of Sparkenhoe Street, St Peter's Road and Gopsall Street in June 1968.

The old Leicester Transport centre in Humberstone Gate. A new one was built in Rutland Street and opened on 22 March 1969 at a cost of £200,000.

High Street in 1969 with Co-operative House the biggest operator on the street. It is now the site of The Shires Shopping Centre.

The Corn Exchange in November 1969 with the old covered roofs of the market stalls in front.

Cheapside in the Market in the 1960s, with the old shops echoing a bygone age.

Not another traffic island! This one sprang up at the junction of Burley's Lane and Abbey Street, near Corah's, in 1960.

St George's Church, off Rutland Street, pictured on a beautiful spring day in 1968.

Sewing machine expert Mr Walter Rollins, who was 74 in 1961, will soon see his historic shop pulled down under a city centre development. His shop sits on the site of the Blue Boar Inn in Highcross Street.

Once Miss Tilly's Mission, these premises were a hardware store and the Elim Pentecostal Church in Ruding Street in the 1960s.

Engelbert Humperdinck became an international singing star in the 1960s. Here we see him when he was plain Gerry Dorsey from Leicester, photographed with fans at the television show *Oh, Boy* in 1957.

The Dallas Boys, from Leicester, were given their first professional contract at £45 per week – £9 a week each – in 1962.

The Bell Hotel, in Humberstone Gate, made way for the Haymarket Shopping Centre.

The former *Evening Mail*
building in London
Road pictured during
the late 1960s.

The Seventies

Bustling High Street in September 1970, in spite of empty shops and difficult parking.

Progress being made – the construction of St Margaret's Way in September 1970.

The Royal Hotel in Horsefair Street, which had been in business for nearly 100 years, announced its closure in February 1971. Everards Brewery Ltd. said it had been precipitated by plans to redevelop by their neighbours, Sun Alliance.

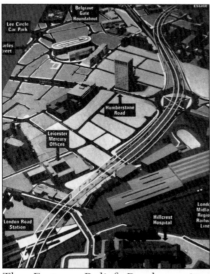

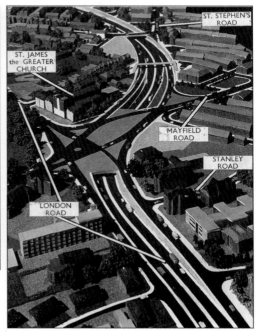

The Eastern Relief Road, a city motorway, as projected in 1971. It would have taken an elevated route from London Road/Mayfield Road to St Matthew's Estate.

Simpkin and James, of Horsefair Street, which closed in February 1971.

Demolition of Belgrave Road Railway Station in February 1972.

Leicester's old fish market, standing as it does a relic of the past, boarded up. The building still survives.

18 Highcross Street, now known as 25 St Nicholas Circle, was saved from demolition and was restored in July 1972. It is believed to have been built by Roger Wyggeston, who was three times Mayor of the town before 1500. Now it is the Costumes Museum.

Kenwood swimming pool, whose owners had applied for planning permission to develop the site for housing in July 1972. Two years later, it became Arreton Close, part of the Kenwood development by Sheriff Construction Company Ltd.

The end of an era in city-centre trading, with the demolition of the old wholesale market around Wigston Street in December 1972.

Robotham's Baby's Kingdom in Belvoir Street, which closed in 1973. The manageress, Mrs Vera Aucott, had been with the store for 49 years.

The County Club building in Market Street. It housed Morgan Squire, a departmental store, in 1973.

Showaddywaddy at the De Montfort Hall in June 1974. The local group had a No. 1 hit in 1976 with *Under The Moon Of Love* which stayed there for three weeks.

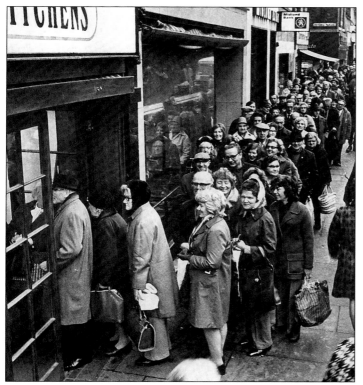

Bread queues . . . one of Leicester's long queues on the morning of 3 December 1974, as the Government attempted to bring a swift end to the bakers' strike.

Main instigators of a High Street plan for a leisure centre was the Co-operative Society in 1974.

The Imperial Hotel, Mere Road, designed by Leicester architect Arthur Wakerley in the 1890s.

The imposing mock Tudor building at the apex of Wellington Street and King Street, which was under threat of demolition in 1975.

The Midland Educational Co. Ltd. took over J.W. Wale & Co., the glass and china business founded by a former Lord Mayor of Leicester, in November 1975, but the firm finally closed in September 1986.

Abbey Park Road on a hot day in July 1976.

St Margaret's Vestry Hall was built between 1866-68 in Humberstone Gate to provide for the sick and poor, supervise street lighting and collect dues for grazing on St Margaret's Pastures and the Abbey Meadows for the parish of St Margaret's. It made way for a block of flats.

Lord Mayor Councillor Bernard Toft opened the new Cheapside pedestrian precinct on 9 May 1977. The ceremony marked the end of months of hard work by Leicester Rotary Club, which paid for the landscaping and the placing of the city's historic High Cross as its centrepiece.

Leicester City FC on tour in Sweden in August 1977. On the bench are: (left to right) Larry May, Carl Jayes, Steve Earle, Ian MacFarlane (in the jacket!), Frank McLintock, Jim Peacock, Steve Bicknell, Peter Welsh, and Winston White.

Leicester v Barbarians on 27 December 1977. Back row (left to right): Ian Smith, Nick Joyce, Peter Wheeler, Steve Newsome, Bill Reichwald, Bob Walker, Robin Cowling, Steve Johnson, Garry Adey, Steve Redfern, Paul Dodge, 'Chalkie' White (coach). Front: Bill Mitchelmore (baggage man), Bleddyn Jones, Dusty Hare, Brian Hall (captain), Steve Kenney, Tim Barnwell, Angus Collington. The result? Tigers lost 12-6.

Victorious Leicestershire County Cricket Club – Ray Illingworth holding the County Championship trophy in September 1977. The players received a limited edition of fine bone china plates to commemorate the county's championship success in 1975.

In October 1979, it was thought the Leicester livestock market could be moved to make way for an industrial estate or a new Granby Halls. The building, with its clock tower, was, however, scheduled for protection.

Built as the Arcadia Electric Theatre in 1910, and designed by Ward and Bell, it later became known as The Cameo Classic Cinema, finally closing its doors in the 1970s.

The new £1 million maternity unit, attached to the Royal Infirmary, was opened on 1 February 1971.

Leicester group Family's farewell concert in September 1973. Roger Chapman and guitarist Jim Cregan are in shot.

Leicester's London Road Railway Station undertook a face lift in 1978 and 1979.

Engelbert's Charity Concert for the Lord Mayor's Scanner Appeal at the De Montfort
Hall in May 1979, was, predictably, a sell-out.